6/6/10

B

Godfrey F
shire whe
studied s~~ocial science~~ ~~ becoming a teacher, and was head of the Religious Studies department in two large comprehensives. Since re-training in counselling and social welfare he has worked in inner city Nottingham and as a specialist in fostering and adoptions in the Derbyshire Dales. His previous books are *Truancy and Social Welfare* (1989) and *Alcohol Among Young People* (1990), both published by the Boys' and Girls' Welfare Society.

GODFREY HOLMES

BEGINNING WHERE I AM

Meditations
for young people

TRIANGLE

First published 1991
Triangle
SPCK
Holy Trinity Church
Marylebone Road
London NW1 4DU

British Library Cataloguing in Publication Data
Holmes, Godfrey *1947–*
    Beginning where I am: meditations for young people.
    1. Christian life – Devotional works
    I. Title
    242

ISBN 0-281-04504-6

Typeset by Inforum Typesetting, Portsmouth
Printed in Great Britain by
BPCC Hazell Books
Aylesbury, Bucks
Member of BPCC Ltd

CONTENTS

WITHIN THESE WALLS

BEYOND THESE WALLS

NOTE: All these meditations can be used both by and about women and men, boys and girls. Just change 'he' into 'she', 'mother' into 'father', and so on.

*Dedicated
to the memory of my mother,
Hilda Florence Ring.
Her voice
made sacred words
sound beautiful and beautiful words
sacred.*

INTRODUCTION

SEEK QUIET WHERE YOU MAY FIND IT

Above the Welsh Borders town of Llangollen on a conical hill stands Castell Dinas Brân. This ancient ruin has a moat, the remains of a tower, arches intact, and even a tunnel. It is an exciting place to visit, lonely and mysterious – made more of an adventure because of a steep walk to reach those rugged stone walls.

I have climbed up to Dinas Brân in all kinds of weather. I have sat on its fortifications when the sky has been blue and the sunshine hot. I have stood there in drenching rain, blown about by fierce icy winds. Yet every time Dinas Brân is a quiet place for me, peaceful in *all* weathers.

Seek quiet where *you* may find it. Think of a favourite place that keeps drawing you back. It might be any river bridge in a town centre, a memorial in a public park, or a summer-house hidden among its trees. You might have a garden at home, or your grand-dad an allotment. Your school might have large playing-fields with a right of way.

Does no one else know about the gravelly track that leads to *your* haven of perfect peace? If that is the case, your meditations will be undisturbed. But if you *are* disturbed, make that interruption part of your meditation.

Your quiet time need not be a pilgrimage. You might find a spare room or a loft upstairs. And if you use your own bedroom for meditation (and many people do), put something on the wall to help your thinking along. Perhaps a poster, or a picture from an out-of-date calendar; or a large print; an ornament or a souvenir from last year's holiday. If you choose a crucifix or a simple wooden cross, consider leaving it up all week.

You might have a special piece of music you want to play before or after meditation. What triggers your emotions and longings? I have used folk-songs such as: 'How can you say you're lonely?' and 'Yesterday'. I have used Elgar's 'Nimrod', and Handel's 'Fireworks Suite'. I particularly like Judy Collins singing: 'Clouds', and a tape of the piano music for the film: 'Elvira Madigan'. Go to any religious book shop and you will find folk gospel tunes, hymns for today, and: 'Jesus Christ Superstar!'

When you seek quiet, think about the quietest time of day. If no other time lends itself, you have your bed. Nobody can stop you thinking, or praying, there. . . . Nor can they find out what you are saying! Then there is the bus stop after breakfast, the traffic jam, and that quarter-of-an-hour after tea. Or you can meditate, and sing with gusto, in your bath.

Some people think deeply whilst they are jogging or digging, sawing a tree trunk or rowing a boat out. I have never had much success meditating and exerting myself at the same time. I *do* find rambling and travelling conducive, however.

Other people have a favourite radio or television programme which gives them the chance to think. Greeting the presenter is like meeting an old friend. Radio 4 has a daily service mid-morning each week-day, and television has God-slots like *Songs of Praise.*

Seek quiet where you may find it.

Perhaps choose a book to help you concentrate. I mention this in the Conclusion. Keep a Bible or a hymn-book near at hand. Don't be afraid to pretend that you are actually sitting in church or in assembly. I know a group who treat their first fruit-juice of the day, their first bread, as a type of Holy Communion. Reverently.

Some young people sit on a bean-bag to think, or on the front door-step. Others lie in a deck-chair, or curl up ready to go to sleep. I like kneeling sometimes, or covering my face with both hands. If it's very dark and nobody's looking, I hold just one hand above my head as if to stop traffic! What posture makes you most comfortable?

Never forget that quietness is also *a state of mind.* Sometimes you will find quietness and tranquillity within yourself when everything outside is noisy and chaotic. But be prepared for having your mind in a state of unease or despair when you're on holiday or out for the day – when you think you *ought* to be happy. Some of life's mysteries are very hard to solve.

Nonetheless, *try* to switch off, and to take time out. Keep doing the work you have been set, or attempt half of it. Enjoy ordinary meetings, ordinary happenings, ordinary television. Quietness – peacefulness – *will* return.

I find it returns quicker if I am not on bad terms with a friend. Broken relationships do cause upset. Equally, making amends, or forgiving someone who has wronged you, brings back a wonderful sense of well-being. What a pity that the word 'Hush!' sounds like a parent or teacher telling us to make less noise. Hush is actually very pleasant:

> With that deep hush subduing all
> The words and works that drown
> The tender whisper of Thy call,
> As noiseless let Thy blessings fall –
> As fell Thy manna down.

3

That call comes to us when we *least* expect it. It beckons us to prayer, and shows us the way when we rise from our meditations, renewed in strength, ready to re-engage in the hurly-burly of daily life.

Jesus chose 'The lone mountain side, before the morning light'. He dragged himself away from a busy ministry, from the pressing crowds, in order to pray – all alone – looking down on the Sea of Galilee.

So must we cherish precious moments of quiet.

Reflection is available to *everyone*, whether they are seated in a cathedral, standing in a country churchyard, paddling on the sea-shore, or wandering along to the post office.

Seek quiet where you may find it.

And when you have found it, return.

MEDITATION

20 QUESTIONS ANSWERED

1. What is the difference between praying and meditating?
Meditating is really only one way of praying, but the way I think of it, prayer is a petition to God: *asking* for something, *praising* God's goodness, or *remembering* someone in particular. Prayer can be structured. Meditation, on the other hand, can be more a journey of the mind, a mental excursion, and it takes its own shape. In practice, there is considerable overlap between the two. In this book, my mental journeys lead in all directions.

2. What is the difference between worrying and meditating?
Worrying is circular. Worries swirl round in the mind, eventually destroying the healthy functioning of the mind. Much mental energy is *wasted* worrying. Of course thinking about it in advance can prepare you for a shock or a setback, just as it can help you move from one point in your life to the next. But try to think of meditation as *a break* from all this. Acknowledge worry. Then move forward.

3. Do I need a religious faith in order to meditate?

Prayer and meditation are both available to you at all stages of belief or unbelief. You may have no *conscious* belief, but still pray to God. On the other hand, you might meet a regular churchgoer with a strong faith who finds meditation very difficult! You can use these meditations whether or not you regularly attend services, school assemblies or youth fellowships.

4. Do I need a God-figure to whom to address my meditations?

Yes – just as you need someone to write to for each letter you write. Address God at the beginning, the middle or the end, or have God in mind all through. Perhaps sit opposite an empty chair. God is *personal* as well as universal. That's why God listens to your smallest concerns, as well as your most difficult problems.

I don't like masculine descriptions of God, with images of power, strength and domination. So I try to use terms like: my Friend, my Comforter, Saviour. Choose the title you like most. 'O God' is not at all irreverent. Try to keep a capital letter for God, as a special dedication.

5. Do I have to have a problem before I can meditate?

No. Meditation is for happy times as well as sad times, for times you want to say nothing as well as for times you want to talk things through. Although you might be perplexed before (or after) using these meditations, you should not associate meditation with things going *wrong*.

6. Do I have to be good in order to meditate?

Again, no. If everybody was good before they could pray or meditate, God would be remote indeed! You do not have to pass any quality threshold. You are valued as you are. You are forgiven whatever you have done. You come.

7. What if I am too busy to meditate?
Find a little space, even just a few moments. Treat meditation as an investment – something that will repay you for time spent. Surround everything you do, all your outings and activities, with spare minutes.

8. What if I am too upset to meditate?
Upset and tears *add* to meditation. With tears in your eyes, still come. In time, your upset will pass. That might take longer than an hour or a day, but keep hoping, keep praying. If you meditate in your *happiest* moments, you will find it easier to approach God in your saddest moments.

9. Do I have to use printed words?
You might be able to meditate easily *without* any printed words. Or you might want printed words to get started. If your memory is good, you will remember printed words without the open page. Or you will recall their gist. I need printed words for inspiration. I discover that inspiration sometimes whilst reading a newspaper or a magazine.

10. Is it wise to speak out loud?
I concentrate more when I talk out loud, even in a mutter or a whisper. The lonelier I am, the louder my voice. There is no right or wrong way. See which suits you better. Space out words with silences.

11. Should I tell other people that I am meditating?
Pehaps not in so many words. Say that you want a bit of time on your own without interruption. Later you may trust a parent or teacher enough to tell him or her about your quiet time. But don't be misunderstood.

12. If my meditation is interrupted, will people think I'm mad?

It is very old-fashioned to think that 'talking to yourself' is madness. It is more likely to be a sign of your sanity! Mental health comes from keeping up a running commentary on how things are going. Think of all those bathroom opera-stars! Never dread interruption. Instead, use it to tell your intruder about God. People will admire your single-mindedness.

13. Should I meditate with other people?

Perhaps not at first. Joint meditation – group meditation – is a wonderful experience, but very different from secluded meditation. The Society of Friends (Quakers) do meditate together. Other groups listen to readings with a silence in between. Most of the following meditations are best said on your own. If you like one, perhaps lend it to a person who might face that same dilemma.

14. What if my mind wanders while I'm meditating?

Let it. Many young people find their minds wander at school, in church and listening to records too. Most printed prayers and meditations give 'leads' to *allow* your mind to wander down other routes. When you have lost concentration, simply look at the view for a while, then come back.

15. What if I go to sleep whilst meditating?

Let sleep come when it will. Welcome sleep. Then meditate again when you awake. If you are *determined* not to droop, then kneel, or sit on an uncomfortable chair! Make sure your last waking thoughts each day are peaceful.

16. Do I need a theme during meditation?

The mind is restless until it finds a river course down

which to run. You might just want to 'stand and stare', without thinking about one particular subject. I like themes, and use themes a lot. But don't ever be *governed* by a theme.

17. Do I need a definite beginning to my meditations?

Most prayers and readings do have beginnings, but meditations can be like magazine articles and start half way through the story! You can then go back (flash-backs) or forward (towards an ending) or stay pondering the ground in between.

First, you can begin with a real-life experience.

Second, you can begin with a real-life incident or observation.

Third, you can begin with a question requiring an answer.

Fourth, you can launch straight in and treat the whole meditation as 'a seamless robe'.

18. Do I need endings to my meditations?

Ideally, the end comes with perfect peace, or the suggestion of a way forward, a way out of difficulty. Or you can end with a question. Often you will reach no conclusion, or you will go back to the beginning. Airing a problem is always useful, however.

19. Are there any word-patterns that are very UNHELPFUL in meditation?

Whatever words suit you, use them.

Word-patterns are very cultural and regional, as well as personal. They are also selective. I like a rhythmic word-pattern, relying on great repetition (usually a near-repeat rather than an exact repeat). Try to avoid very long rambling sentences. Avoid also very long words or words that jar. Avoid upsetting, hateful words. They are very destructive. Certainly express all your hurt, but move on from that hurt. Never try to make words rhyme when they don't! You can meditate with or without your own poetry, with or without other people's poetry.

20. *Do I grow out of meditating?*
Never. Even on the proverbial deathbed, please go on meditating. There is nothing childish or wishy-washy about meditation. On the other hand, you might grow beyond *these* meditations. God will always listen to you, throughout your life.

USING THESE MEDITATIONS

Not everything in this book can mean something to everyone all of the time. So you can pick and choose from these meditations ones that suit you.

You can also change the words freely to make them your own. You may need to cut out bits that don't apply to you, and put in bits that *do* apply.

No two meditations are the same, so you can use a piece about your father to talk about your mother, or a piece about your girlfriend to talk about your boyfriend.

Feel free to add or take away an 's' when talking about brothers, sisters, parents, and so on. Change his to her, school to college, work to school, and put in different people's names – as you like, to fit your own situation.

Group use

Most of these meditations have been designed for individual use, to fit in with the idea of someone beginning to look at a very personal concern. They can be used in groups though. Where group leaders are considering one of these meditations they may want to re-write it. This allows them to make small changes, like 'I' to 'we', and to add sentences which might apply to one of the group, or to miss out sentences which might upset one of the group. If the script is used as it is, leaders might want to introduce it as a cry from the heart of an imaginary teenager, someone who is not indentical to any one member of that particular group, but someone whom every member of that group would *recognise*.

Making up meditations on your own

It is almost impossible to advise anyone how to devise one of these meditations from scratch, because my words are not your words, and my style is not your style. You can, though, confidently write a meditation which will take you in the same direction as one of mine.

Unclutter your mind.

Place a blank sheet of paper in front of you.

Write a title of five or six words, starting with 'I . . .' or 'A Meditation on . . .'

Don't mix subjects. There is no need to aim for great length, or to try to impress God with cleverness. Don't redraft, or go into ten editions. Instead stick to about twenty separate lines, one line leading on naturally to the next. Include *forbidden* thoughts, *forgotten* griefs.

Read your meditation through twice, *very* slowly. *And keep it.*

Treating subjects you have never experienced

Whenever you read a story or a novel you are meeting a situation at second hand. The same is true of most plays and poems, including TV soap operas. You might have been through something similar. That's why the script reminds you of past feelings, but it is very unlikely that the writer is copying exactly your experience.

Don't hesitate to use your imagination along with your sympathy. For instance, if you are getting on very well with your mother and you choose the meditation of a person saddened at their parent's rejection, you could start with the words:

'O God, I am so lucky . . . It is not always like this . . .' or 'O God, I used to think this . . . I've moved on now . . . but my friends are not so lucky . . .'

Try putting an empty pair of shoes next to your bed or chair. Keep looking down on these shoes as if you had to place yourself in that other person's shoes.

Another way of transferring yourself in time and circumstance is to place an object next to this book as you read part of it. If the subject is smoking, look at an empty cigarette packet. If the subject is complaint, read a guarantee from your hair-dryer before going through the meditation.

PART ONE

BEGINNING WHERE I AM

I AM DEPRESSED

O God, my Comforter . . .
If You want to know what it's like to be depressed,
Look at me.
When others are happy,
I am sad;
When others are active,
I am passive;
When others are keen,
I am half-hearted.
Depression is waiting for me
round every corner . . .
It is the cloud that hides the sun;
it is the ghost that haunts me;
it is the shadow I cannot escape.
I know that other people become depressed.
But their depression doesn't last.
Mine *does*.
Their depression can be explained;
mine has neither rhyme nor reason.
Their depression can be shrugged off;
mine never moves far away.
When I am *not* depressed,

I wonder when I shall be.
I want to drown my depression
so that it cannot surface.
I want to suffocate my depression
so that it cannot breathe.
I want to side-track my depression
so that it cannot get back on course.
My depression has cornered me so often.
How can I now turn and face it?
How can I make friends with it . . .
without being swallowed up by it?

What do You say?
Listening to You won't be time wasted.
Stay with me through the dark night
of my depression . . .
until I see daylight at the other end.
Then I shall control my depression
where once it controlled me.

I DO NOT LIKE MY OWN COMPANY

My Comforter,
I don't know whether anybody else has this problem.
I rather think not, because I keep telling myself
it's not natural.
You see, I don't like my own company.
I can't manage to be on my own for long spells.
I do not think highly enough of myself
to live with myself;
I'm not content enough with my own company
to stay in my own company.
That is why I always try to avoid being on my own –
and yet, so that I can hide my problem,
I stay up in my bedroom when I could be in the lounge;
I go out on my own when other people
ask me to go with them;
I turn down dates; or else,
I make no effort to arrange them.
There must be lots of
people who'd *like* to go out with me,
and it needn't lead to anything serious!
I am very good now at hiding my problem.
I manage to be all on my own
when that's the last thing I want,
and nobody's got a clue.
They imagine I must be happy
because that's what I tell my family;
that's what I tell my friends.
But I'm ever so miserable on my own.
I waste a lot of time and energy just longing
not to be on my own.
I keep thinking what my family and friends
are doing without me.
Perhaps I'm a bit of a martyr . . .

I'm punishing myself.

Please be my Companion in this miserable state,
and now I have told You the truth,
help me to find one other person I can tell.
Then I can begin to balance
half my time alone, and half with others.
And give me a good book, or some good music
or a re-shuffled bedroom
so that I start to really look forward
to times when I'm on my own.

I CAN'T THINK STRAIGHT

I went into this newsagent's today.
There was a whole shelf full of fat puzzle books:
Puzzles for the beach and the bus and the bathroom:
Crosswords, riddles and teasers . . .
Clues to discover, numbers to multiply.
Do all these puzzles do anything for me?
I can't think straight at present, God.
So I read by just skimming the pages.
I grab a newspaper just for the headlines.
I pick up a comic strip.
So I'm not actually stretching my mind.
I used to think a lot more logically.
People even called me 'outspoken',
because of my strong views –
but not now. I can't say anything much now.
Trivial details clutter up my mind,
and useless worries.
I switch off in lessons at school –
Then I switch on the television at home.
I watch whatever is on,
zapping from soaps to second-rate comedies.
I feel I *want* to concentrate more . . .
I want to worship You, God.
And I want to support my friends
when they are in trouble.
I just need to be clearer in my mind,
so my mind and my body both act swiftly.
If my mind wanders any more, openings will close
and celebrations will happen
with me on the pavement outside . . . looking in.

I CAN'T BUILD UP MUCH ENTHUSIASM

O God,
I've been a bit of a wet blanket of late.
Friends come up with bright ideas,
but I shut my ears.
They suggest interesting places where we might go,
but I stay where I am.
My brothers and sisters come
to show me their paintings,
their models, their toys –
but I ignore them because it's the middle
of my favourite programme.
My mother thinks of a juicy bit of gossip,
and I say 'So what?'
My father boasts about his sporting triumphs.
I groan and mutter: 'Hole in one?'
Grand-dad goes on about the war
and all his medals.
I sing old marching songs,
and 'Onward Christian Soldiers!'
My grandma goes on about her girlhood –
fetching in the zinc tub
from the coalshed, and darning socks.
Mockingly, I play an imaginary violin.
Or else a neighbour comes round
to show slides of a holiday overseas.
I yawn and then ask lots of silly questions.
I'm not one to get all that excited about anything.
Friends are hooked on fashion or football
or clothes or computers.
None of that sparks me off.
I pretend to concentrate
when my mind is miles away.
Highs and lows become straight lines;

jokes mis-fire; holidays are boring;
and pleasant surprises do not surprise me.

O Redeemer: when days are flat, give me height;
when days have sparkle, give them
length;
when my thoughts are narrow, give me
breadth;
and when my thoughts are shallow, give
them depth.

I'M UNSURE OF MY BELIEFS

O God, I hear adults who are much surer
of their beliefs than I am.
They sing: 'I will trust in Him!'
They sing: 'What a Friend we have in Jesus!'
They sing: 'Great is Thy faithfulness!'
They sing: 'Hosanna in the Highest Heaven!'
Maybe these folk have doubts,
but they do not betray them.
Maybe these folk have questions,
but they do not ask them.
I cannot match their devotion,
but I do believe in You.

And there are many people of my own age
who are much surer of their beliefs than I am.
They too sing Gospel songs and choruses.
They follow Bible study-notes,
and go to *extra* services.
They say their prayers
more regularly than I do,
and they talk about their beliefs
more openly than I do.
I cannot match their devotion,
but I do believe in You.

My faith is still in its infancy.
It's full of contradictions –
I could be called a hypocrite.
I think twice before I become committed –
indeed, I step back rather than admit
having any commitment.
I am afraid of taunts and jibes.

I am afraid of clever debating points
I shall not be able to field.
People might laugh at me, or keep away from me,
if I say I believe in You.

And those at home who know me very well
might turn round and say my holiness is just
a flash in the pan.
My little faith might collapse
like a house of cards . . .
so that I'm further away from You
than when I first came to You.
I'm not a very good disciple . . .
but I do believe in You.

I'VE DONE SOMETHING WHICH CANNOT BE FORGIVEN

Thousands of people must be living
normal lives, going about their
daily business, unsuspecting and unsuspected . . .
and yet they are perpetually plagued by
the memory of something they have done . . .
still unconfessed . . . and they cannot
share the burden with anyone.
The shadow is dark indeed;
the torment is terrifying.

I know because *I* have done something
which cannot be forgiven.
It was something very bad,
very thoughtless.
It could have hurt a lot of people . . .
I do not know exactly whom.
It could have mystified people
and wasted their time.
It could have led to something
too horrific for me to contemplate
then or now.
Yet I went undiscovered.
Many of the words and thoughts and deeds
that are beyond forgiveness
do go undiscovered . . .
known only to the person responsible.
The law is built
on a framework of reporting yourself,
of pleading or confessing,
of being detected or being caught red-handed.
Most crimes remain known only

to those who have committed them . . .discovery is
    almost impossible . . .
the offender hoards the secret.
I wish I *had* been discovered . . .
I wish I could confess now . . .
but it is too late.
In the Bible I found it was possible
to 'sin against the Holy Spirit'
and that offence – whatever it is or was –
sounds equally unforgivable.
I can just tell You, my Friend . . .
holding nothing back.

I WONDER WHY I WAS BORN

They'll always say of me:
'Born in 19--'.
That must be very important:
the beginning of my existence . . .
perpetually remembered, every birthday,
every time a register is called,
every time there are forms to be filled in.
My birth – my date of birth –
my place of birth – my means of birth –
my weight at birth – my birthday suit.
Were my parents overjoyed at the happy event?
And my grand-parents too?
Did nurses and midwives crowd round my cot?
Did they hang up balloons and festoons when I –
the newest arrival – arrived back home?
My birth was the beginning of me as I am . . .
foreshadowed some months ahead
by the union of two bodies –
or two test tubes – to achieve my conception.
I could have been born to two different people,
in a different country, in a different decade.
I could have been born either richer or poorer,
the same sex or the opposite sex,
with a personality more agreeable
or more disagreeable!
I could even have been still-born,
or miscarried . . .
or born too frail to survive
my first few hours, my first few days.

But I was born as I was when I was . . .
and now I suppose
I should not question the event of my birth . . .

its timing, its motivation, its implications . . .
because I am as I am.

But the question still lingers in the back of my mind:
O God, why was I born?

PART TWO

PACKAGING MYSELF

I DON'T LOOK LIKE I WANT TO LOOK

When I look round at other people of my age,
they always look much better than I do.
Everyone else loses weight when they want to,
or gains it when they want to – not me.
I am covered with spots; their skin is clear.
My body has a shape, but it's not *the right* shape;
My hair has a style, but it's not *the right* style.
My clothes are smart, but not very fashionable:
I always look as if I came out of a clothes shop
two years ago.
I couldn't look glamorous even if I had
my own designer.
My friends think I'm odd.
When they're not laughing at me,
I feel that they want to.
Yet I have tried – *You* know – to look good.
I seem to have spent ages in front of a mirror.
I have bought all sorts of creams and gels and powders.
I have trekked round all the posh shops
and nearly got thrown out of some of them.
I have fussed; I have fiddled; I have fretted.
If I asked friends how I looked, I'd give them a field day.
O God, I want to *like* how I look –

to be so pleased with how I look
that I can forget how I look.

Maybe it isn't worth bothering about
my appearance: people seem happiest at the seaside
where appearances don't matter so much.
Make me just a bit contented,
so that I can then, at least, boast about
being different from everybody else.

I DO THE THINGS I SHOULDN'T DO

O God, why do I do the things I shouldn't do?
I have lived long enough to know
what I should avoid doing.
I have said to myself often enough:
'That'll get me into trouble', or
'That's plain daft'.
I have seen my parents and my teachers
and my friends – all making mistakes.
I have read in the newspapers about complete strangers
making the same mistakes – or different ones.
Sometimes I've been quite chuffed to find
other people doing what they ought not to
or not doing what they ought to.
I have laughed at them,
and waited for them to slip up.
If they had been perfect,
it would have made me imperfect . . .
Perhaps it is time for me to face up to something.
I have teachers to teach me lessons.
I have the sort of family who will help out.
I have street-wise youth leaders.
I've even got the Agony Aunts –
if I can keep a straight face.
Then I have the Bible – Your particular signal.
I can search out saints who used to be sinners –
and sinners who used to be saints.
But I still do the things I shouldn't do –
What is the answer to this one?

I SAY THE THINGS I SHOULDN'T SAY

O God! I wish I didn't open my mouth –
Then I wouldn't need to shut it so quickly.
My words often hurt or deceive other people.
And once my words are spoken, I can't take them back.
When my words should be comforting, they are
   upsetting.
When my words should be cheerful, they are grumpy.
When I should be the peace-maker,
I throw fat on the fire.
Some days I chatter emptily – jabbering away
when my family and friends want silence –
when they want *me* to listen to them.
My tongue is a nuisance.
It wakes when scandal is around –
Then it will not sleep again
until misunderstandings abound.
If words are like arrows
my tongue is a quiver full of them.
I save all my most hurtful words
for times they will strike target.
Even my gossip is hardly innocent:
I pretend to be inquiring when I am really probing.
I gossip to spread intrigue –
then I stand well away to listen
to my careless words causing astonishment.
If only I could guard my mouth like a fortress.
If only I could stop making excuses
for my wagging tongue.
If only I could stop saying
what comes into my mind first of all.
Help me O God to handle words as carefully
as one pound coins,
and let none of them be any less in value.

I HAVE BEEN TELLING LIES

Today I told a little lie.
Then I told a bigger lie
to cover my little lie.
I tell lies throughout each school day
to explain why I have not done the work
I ought to have done.
I tell lies to keep the friends I have
and to keep alive the wishes I ought not to have.
I recall happenings which have not happened.
I invent people I have not met.
I imagine a little world . . .
a little world I can live in
full of things I have not done,
wiped clean of things I *have* done.
I tell lies at home, to the rest of my family.
I tell some lies to save me from punishment . . .
and other lies to safeguard my freedom.
I tell still more lies to safeguard my sanity.
I am not quite sure, my Redeemer,
which of my tales is a lie . . .
and which is the truth . . . or part of the truth.
Perhaps the truth is simply all the lies
that have not yet been found out as untrue!
Some mornings I get up determined not to lie.
But then I tell a little lie
when asked why I lied the day before.
I *could* stop lying forever . . .
but then everybody who was not expecting me
to tell the truth
would think that I was still lying!
But I need not to lie to YOU:
the Way, the Truth and the Life.
I need not lie to You because You exist

in a world where people can face up to the truth
and not be afraid of the truth.

Show me now the way to that Truth
which is hidden from me.
Then I shall find Life.
My life will be one where I do not need
to hide the truth from others.
Really, the Truth shall make me free.

I'M NOT VERY ORGANISED

I don't seem to be very organised, my Friend.
In fact, I'm very disorganised.
I think
'I'll write a letter' – then I can't be bothered.
'I'll do some homework' – then I can't be bothered.
'I'll sort through my drawers' – then I can't be bothered.
I pile books and papers in one big heap.
I mix my clean and my dirty washing.
I go out without a coat;
I study without the right books.
I tell friends I'll meet them – and arrive too late;
I tell my parents I'll be in at 10 – and arrive too late.
I go to town shopping and buy things I don't need.
I leave shampooing my hair till it itches.
I avoid going to the dentist or the optician.
I'm sleepy when I need to be awake,
and awake when I need to be sleepy.
I *want* to find a few moments each day
to think and to pray
and to keep my diary up to date.
I don't seem to be achieving very much –
certainly not as much as other people in my group.
Please give me a thorough re-organisation,
So that I put first things first
and last things last.
Give me plenty of time for the things that matter,
and make sure, my Friend,
that I stick to my good intentions,
and stay one step ahead of myself,
not two steps behind.

I HAVE STARTED SMOKING

I have started to smoke.
I always knew people who smoked.
Some of my best friends
have been smokers for ages.
But up till now I have not wanted to join in.
Then came exams, combined with
a build up of disagreements here at home.
Now I am smoking quite regularly.
I am paying for the habit in money . . .
I am even borrowing money.
I am paying for the habit in other ways too
unless I can stop smoking . . .
which I find I can't do.
I used to think smoking was senseless.
I didn't like the look of drooping cigarettes . . .
or the smell, or the fog,
or the tar stains on the fingers.
I used to think people were stupid
not to give up smoking
at the very first chance they had . . .
especially when they were relaxed,
and on holiday, and in good company.
Now I belong to that small company
of hardened smokers . . .
so that I rarely refuse a cigarette.
I look forward to the walk home from school,
the walk after tea,
the break between classes,
when I shall be able to light up.
I know I can live without tobacco
because I used to live without tobacco.
I know that even smoking
just three cigarettes a day,

I shall get through another fifty thousand
in my shortened lifetime.

O, my Saviour, save me from this habit.
Light up my life in such a way
that the little gold and silver boxes
will stay right there
in the shops that shouldn't have
sold them to me.

I HAVE STARTED DRINKING MORE

I have started to drink beer and cider.
I like a Martini or a glass of sherry.
It's not surprising that I should admit this.
Everybody drinks.
It is socially acceptable to drink.
Everybody puts pressure on everybody else to drink.
It would only be remarkable
if I turned down alcohol.
I did use to turn down alcohol.
After a couple of furtive drinks at home . . .
a tin of shandy at school . . .
a glass of sparkling wine at a wedding . . .
I used to prefer soft drinks.
I bought soft drinks;
I was offered soft drinks.
Now I buy strong drinks;
I am offered strong drinks.
The easiest option for me
would be to become a social drinker
just like everybody else:
not an alcoholic . . .
just a drinker of alcohol
when all my friends drink alcohol
a drinker of alcohol
when my colleagues at work drink alcohol
a drinker of alcohol at college,
at a party . . . after a big match.
The reason I do tell You, my Friend,
about my drinking
is that I'm not *certain* it's right.
I don't know that I'm helping myself by drinking
or that I'm setting a good example.
People special in my life drink . . .

but maybe they are waiting for me to stop drinking
so that they can follow my example.
I don't *need* this alcohol.
They don't need this alcohol.
Make me brave to hold my ground
till this tide of alcohol turns.

I AM EATING TOO MUCH

Whenever food is served,
I want to be served more than anyone else.
Whenever food is set out on a table . . .
I want to take more than anyone else.
Whenever food is on offer,
I say that 'I'm starving!'
Whenever food is set out on a different table,
somewhere else,
I go in search of it.
Food is my passion, my craving.
Food is the centrepiece of my life.
I live for the next meal,
then come back for seconds.
I live for the next feast,
then I gobble it up by the plateful.
And, if no meal is planned,
if no meal is prepared,
I eat snacks between meals,
sweet and sticky snacks,
cakes and biscuits, left-overs, take-aways.
I gorge myself till I'm almost too full
for the actual meal . . .
Then everybody is astonished when I say:
'I'm not hungry.'
I keep promising myself I will eat less.
Or I will eat more of what is less fattening.
I keep meaning to start a diet.
I will cut back after this one treat,
this one extra helping,
this one party . . .
and I promise myself a reward of something tasty
in return for turning down something tasty!
So far, my weight has not soared too much . . .

but it will.
As yet, my family have not detected my bingeing . . .
but they will.
Then all the ugly consequences of my greed will be out
for all to see.

I know I'm greedy; I know I'm a pig.
But I keep saying it will be all right:
'Something came over me.'
'It'll all be different in a couple of days . . . You see!'
Well, You *do* see.
You see that food is the false God in my life,
waiting to be dethroned.

I DON'T WANT TO MAKE THIS COMPLAINT

'Goods may not be exchanged.'
'No refunds given.'
'All complaints must be directed to Head Office.'
'We don't make the rules . . .
we're here to enforce them.'
O God, so many obstacles are put up to prevent
me making a complaint. However good my case,
I have to run an obstacle race.
Shop-keepers put up obstacles
just to stop me complaining.
They make me look silly to complain.
They tell me I did not read the instructions.
They make it look as if I am at fault, not they.
They tell me they've never had
a single complaint before mine.
I am *not* a very assertive person, my Friend.
I know what I want, but not how to get it.
I know the words I want to use . . .
but I do not remember them until it is too late . . .
until I have been made to look like a fool
or a persistent moaner or a time-waster.
Worse, most places don't have
any complaints procedure at all.
It's ever so hard to complain
about teachers or doctors,
about policemen or social workers.
They are believed because they're in authority.
I have no authority and I am not believed.
I *have* been wronged; I have been badly treated –
but I don't want to make this complaint.

PART THREE

ENDING UP

I HAVE NO AMBITION

My Friend,
I come to You to talk about ambition.
Ambition wants first of all to grow up –
to be an adult.
Ambition wants to pass exams, to travel –
camping, hitching, backpacking . . .
treading where human foot has never trod before.
Above all, ambition wants a job –
some children long to nurse sick people;
or to drive enormous cranes –
ambition wants to go much further.
After getting a job,
ambition wants a responsible job;
and then the *most* responsible job;
and then the *highest-paid* job.
Not yet content, ambition wants a home of its own:
a semi with new carpets and furniture.
Ambition then looks for a detached house
with the deepest carpets,
the plushest furniture.
And when ambition wants a family of its own,
it looks for a partner

and two children,
a second more exciting partner
and two brighter children.

Well, I lack ambition.
If something's attractive,
it's soon unattractive.
If something's a challenge,
it's soon not worth the candle.
If something's irresistible,
I soon find I can live without it.
I do not want to collect
honours and certificates and antiques.
I do not want to get too far in life
too quickly.
I do not want to waste time and energy
keeping up with the pack.
Help me, O God, to enjoy the present
more than the future –
I want to see Your plans for me *now*,
not just Your design for my future.

I DON'T WANT A LIFE OF DRUDGERY

O God, I have met so many
dull people in my time . . .
so many drudges.
Grim-faced, they set about their daily jobs
of washing, cleaning, shopping and bed-making.
When that round is over . . .
they begin all over again:
ironing, hoovering and doing the pots.
So many lives are a drab routine of
work, eat, sleep . . .
I want my life to be different.
I'll do my fair share of chores.
I don't really mind helping round the house.
And on holiday, little jobs don't seem boring.
And I don't mind if I'm being *paid*
for cooking and cleaning.
A lot of my friends *are* paid for these.
The pay is terrible, but this type of job
is the easiest to get:
part-time, seasonal, and by the hour.
I once read about Martha and Mary in the Bible.
Mary sat at Jesus' feet listening intently,
while Martha was behind the scenes cooking!
I would rather be a Mary than a Martha.
I don't want to miss interesting conversation,
exciting matches on television, and outings,
just to finish routine jobs.
Nor do I want to marry somebody who leaves me
to do all the housework.
I'm worried I might always be taken for granted.
Saviour, save me from drudgery!

I DON'T WANT TO LOOK FOR WORK

My careers teacher told me to look for work.
My parents told me to look for work.
The Job Centre told me to look for work –
but it's not that easy, my Guide and Friend.
There's not much work about around here,
and the jobs that are there are badly paid.
Even so, I *would* look for work –
but it's not that easy, my Guide and Friend.
You know I have other things on my mind at present:
the search for a flat or bed-sitter of my own,
getting fitter, restoring my health,
and building up a new relationship
now that my best friend has deserted me.
I need a few months to sort myself out –
but it's not that easy, my Guide and my Friend.
The Job Centre wants me to join a Job Club.
They insist that I go for all these interviews,
and traipse round from factory to factory asking
for a vacancy that won't exist for the next ten years.
They want me to make lots of 'phone calls
as soon as the paper is published on a Thursday –
but it's not that easy, my Guide and my Friend.
I suppose I could become *self*-employed.
I could make my hobby into my living.
I could get by on some payments
and bridging benefits.
I could move to London,
to the South-East corner –
but it's not that easy, my Guide and my Friend.

I DON'T WANT TO START WORK

I come to You, my Protector,
at the break of this new day
because I do not want to go to work.
I might be given jobs I cannot do.
I might meet fellow-workers I do not like.
Some of the work will be dirty and messy.
Or it might be very tricky.
Or plain boring.
I have had a space since last working for money.
And when I last worked for money,
I was more in control than now.
And it was fewer hours.
I could leave one part-time job and walk into another.
I cannot do that now.
I have already signed along the dotted line.
I have agreed to lots of small print.
I might break something, or break some rule.
I might arrive late, or not be able to leave early.
I might lose an important piece of paper.
I might have my work handed back to me
to do again. The others will complain
that I am slowing them down . . .
I have heard of bullying by workers, supervisors,
bosses and union officials;
I have heard of initiation ceremonies,
as well as golden hand-shakes.
Some people leave work with a spring in their step . . .
Others leave worn out.
I just don't know what today has in store for me.
If I forget You, please don't forget me.

I DON'T WANT TO MOVE INTO A FLAT OF MY OWN

I'm coming back to You, my Refuge,
because I am about to move into a place of my own . . .
and I'm beginning to have second thoughts.
I sit here in my old bedroom
looking round at all my packed boxes –
gazing nostalgically out of the window.
I want now to stay with my family and my memories.
Please help me to make the break.
I am ready *in age*, but unready in feelings.
The flat I have chosen has four walls –
four bare, blank walls compared with *these* walls.
My furniture and cases will get there, but
I will have left my past behind.
I'm sure my parents will want to visit me.
I'm sure my friends will want to visit me.
My flat will be cosy –
and I shall dish out curry and coffee.
They'll all say: 'How nice!' – to make me grin.
But when they go, they will leave a lump in my throat.
Should I unpack all my belongings now, my Friend?
Should I cancel my tenancy agreement,
and re-possess this room?
Can I stay just a few months longer –
because I am so unprepared . . .
for all that washing, and cooking,
and cleaning, and paying of bills?
No. I shall move into the flat
that was someone else's – and make it my own.
I'll have new freedom,
and the chance to think for myself.
I'm a bit frightened, but also quite excited.
I'll meet You there: my Comforter, my Companion.

I DON'T WANT TO BECOME A DRUG ADDICT

I guess it can do no harm:
this little purple-heart.
I guess it can do no harm: this magic mushroom,
this filter paper full of pot.
Others guess it can do them no harm
when they accept drugged sugar lumps
and little tinfoil packages full of crack.
They guess just one shot of heroin
will make them cope better
with all their troubles.
I have been offered hard drugs
and I have been able to turn them down.
Other people have been offered the same drugs
and have not been able to turn them down . . . so
they have borrowed and stolen so
they can pay for more drugs . . . so
they are now addicted . . .
and their lives are in tatters.
Other people have used second-hand needles;
they are dying of AIDS.
Drugs have overwhelmed them; drugs have wiped out
their chance of living without drugs.
O, my Companion, I *can* live without drugs.
because I have a good family and a stable home.
And I have the willpower to live without drugs.
I have known where to stop,
and I have known other people in my circle
ready to say NO.
Should I tell the police
that I've been offered drugs again?
Perhaps a smooth character in sunglasses
will draw his limousine
right up beside me in the street . . .

and make me an offer that this time I *cannot* refuse.
O God, how I hate this drugs traffic.

I DON'T WANT TO DIE

O God, I don't want to think about death.
Death angers me
just as life amazes me.
I know the world existed for centuries
before I was born
and will continue to exist for centuries
after I'm gone.
At present I occupy the little gap in between.
I live because I was given the 'gift of life'.
Yet nobody told me this was a gift
that could be taken back
by the first drunken driver meandering along;
by the first heavy lorry thundering past my home;
by the first outbreak of meningitis;
by cancer and by all manner of dangerous diseases;
by a boat going down or an aeroplane crashing;
or by the first hot-headed terrorist
putting his case before all others.
I wonder whether elderly people still want
to possess 'the gift of life'.
I wonder whether any of them want
to give that gift back to its Maker –
or are they just resigned to their fate?
Do they just fritter away the hours and days
as many people – much younger –
fritter away *their* hours and days?
Do they look back on a life crowned with glory,
or one racked with pain, shortened by heartbreak?
O God, my years may be few or many.
You are my Comforter.
Comfort me now as I protest:
I don't want to die.

PART FOUR

WITHIN THESE WALLS

MY MUM IS SO BUSY

I want more of my mum's time.
I want more of her attention.
I want to test out some of my theories;
I want to confirm some of my observations;
I want to talk over some of my problems.
I want there to be a parent on hand . . .
because I am not yet self-sufficient.
Besides,
I think there *ought* to be a parent in the wings.
My mum decided to add me to a family;
My mum knows me better than anyone else does;
My mum manages to see things in perspective –
despite my doubts and my dissent.
Yet she is ever so busy.
There is work to go to,
or there is a stream of telephone calls
to be answered.
There are the accounts to be balanced,
or there are too many alterations to the house
to be completed.
There is shift-work or there is piece-work
or there is work brought back from the office

to do on the kitchen table.
There are all the demands of my younger brother
or sister to attend to.
Then there are her own interests and hobbies —
her music, her clubs,
her sporting achievements.
She has different friends to visit
or to be visited by . . .
and shops to go shopping to . . .
and the garden needing gardening . . .
and the motor needing a mechanic.
My God, You are always with me, but
where do *I* fit into their scheme of things?

I'M NOT GETTING ON WELL WITH MY PARENTS

My Friend:
Today I have a very common problem to bring You:
I'm not getting on very well with my parents.
Every day I grow further away from them.
They say they're suggesting – I call it nagging;
they say they're advising – I call it criticizing;
they say 'We're only warning you' –
when they've gone right over the top.
So many days they just don't understand me.

I'm not allowed to make my own choices –
not even my own mistakes.
If I go around with someone
they decide they much prefer someone else;
if I take up one hobby,
they feel sure I'd really be happier with another;
if I start one chore –
they draw up a whole list of them.
They'd even control my TV –
if I handed over the remote control.
So many days they're watching my every move . . .
telling me how they'd manage my life
so much better than I do.

They plague me with questions
and I can't find the right words to answer
so I say nothing – and then I'm 'stubborn'.
My time doesn't seem to go by their clock;
my hopes and theirs just don't tie up.
We don't often get into full-scale conflict,
but we do seem to be sniping at each other
from our opposite camps –

not out on the battlefield,
clearing the air with a thundering row.

My God, I think they mean well . . .
I know I mean well.
One thing surprises me:
when I get to understand
(just a little bit every now and then)
what makes them tick . . .

then I feel I'm on your wavelength too.

Is it just that
everyone likes to be appreciated?

MY PARENTS SHOUT AT ME

I come to You, my Comforter,
because my parents shout at me –
And if they are not shouting at me,
they are snapping at me
often over tiny failings,
tiny happenings,
tiny misunderstandings.
And I am tempted to shout back.
It all starts on a low key
when I ask a question or make a suggestion.
They do not want to answer my question
or to follow my suggestion.
We disagree, but we do not *agree* to disagree.
I try to restate my position.
Then they restate *their* position.
None of us will climb down, so we clash.
They are not prepared to budge,
even though I am being reasonable.
I say that
I will go ahead even without their permission.
My parents reply that
they will stop me whatever I do, wherever I go.
Then they start shouting at me.
I soon get upset because
basically I'm a quiet person.
I want to live and let live.
I like to be heard,
and I'm usually flexible.
I prefer peace and quiet to disruption.
I want to be friendly towards my parents.
But they intimidate me.
I do not want to swear at my parents –
not even behind their backs.

But their shouting gets on my nerves.
My father blows his top and follows me upstairs —
still shouting.
Meanwhile my mother cools down and cries:
'What will the neighbours think?'
I don't know what the neighbours think,
but I know what *I* think.

O God, I hate to hear my parents shouting at me.
I wish I could tell them that . . .
in the lowest possible voice.
I wish I could whisper Your words:
that Perfect Love Casts Out Fear.

I CAN HEAR MY PARENTS QUARRELLING

I can hear the sound of raised voices.
I can hear the sounds — but not the words.
That is why I am here.
I used to listen to the actual words.
I was there behind the door:
hoping to find out what I
was not supposed to hear —
yet hoping not to be found out.
I can hear raised voices . . .
voices charged with emotion . . .
emotions charged with anger — anger and bitterness.
I don't want to hear any more.
That is why I am here.
These quarrels take a few days to build up . . .
and a few more days to die down.
Now it's money. Now it's what they suspect.
Now it's blame:
   'You don't understand me.'
   'You don't care what I think.'
   'You're always on at me . . . and I HATE you!'
Well, my Friend, if they hate each other,
why do they stay? . . .
except to argue, and to torment each other!
You have some of the answers
because You are listening too.
There are days when *I* quarrel . . .
and that makes me feel worse today.
My quarrels are silly — where theirs are serious.
My quarrels are sudden —
where theirs seem to be planned . . .
almost to a script,
a script that cannot be changed.
Very soon, I know one parent will make

a dramatic gesture:
one or other of them will throw something,
hit something . . . hit someONE!
One or other of them will make a stormy exit . . .
just like the script says.
Only . . . I do not want to see this play.
I want the volume of their voices turned down.
Nobody will say: 'Good Night!' to me tonight.
They never do after one of their quarrels.
Let me settle to hear Your words instead.

I CAN'T GET ON WITH MY STEPMOTHER

O God,
some things I don't fully understand:
divorce and re-marriage,
widowhood and living together.
I am beginning to feel the results of
some children's need for a 'substitute parent'.
I now have a stepparent
– a stepping-in parent –
and I can't get on with this new figure in my life.
There I was, living my own life, doing my own thing . . .
when along came an additional mother,
a strange adult –
who wanted a say in my affairs,
some control; who wanted to interfere.
This person even wants to alter the way
we run the household.
Secretly,
I prefer to be left to my own devices.
I do not want a new character charming my dad . . .
offering to help pay the bills,
to mend what is torn or broken,
and to care *for us*.
I do not want extra gifts, extra clothes,
extra treats, extra outings.
I do not want to be bought out
like some failed business.
I do not want *my life* torn or broken.
I cannot transfer my loyalty
– at least not yet – my Friend.
I want to be able to make up my own mind
about this person . . .
and from what I've seen already,
I'm not all that impressed.

My former full-time mum had faults . . .
but nothing to compare with this one's faults.
My departed mum had expectations –
but they were not unreasonable and unreachable
like this one's expectations.
My *real* mum used to get angry –
but at least I listened.

Why should I like a person whose parenthood
is untried and untested,
except in some other way
– in someone else's home –
where she wasn't all that successful?
This new mum is irrelevant . . .
Or is she?

I MISS MY DAD NOW HE HAS LEFT

One parent has now left.
He has departed, escaped, fled.
The door of our home has drawn to –
leaving him on the other side.
I suppose we could see it coming.
There have been hints and clues,
unexplained absences.
There was early talk of a reconciliation.
an attempt to breathe new life into the marriage,
the suggestion of new joint interests,
talking problems through as they came up,
not weeks later;
sharing more, trusting more,
enjoying the children more.
But all that came to an abrupt end
and he left . . . with a car full of keepsakes.
Of course, there will be occasional
or renewed contacts;
there will be birthday cards
and Christmas presents;
there will be access visits
and overnight stays.
There will be agreed settlements
and contested settlements,
but it will not be the same.
We may not have seen so much of him recently . . .
but at least he was there in the background.
Now he is part of another household,
another building, another neighbourhood,
another Church, another *family*.
There will be fewer – if any – occasions
when we can all sit round together . . .
and laugh . . . and tease each other. . .

and watch videos . . . and go on outings . . .
like we used to before storm-clouds gathered.
Mum and Dad were once happy
just with each other, but not now.
The photographs are still in their frames;
the places at table are all laid,
but . . . I need no longer ask over the banister:
'Is that you?'
O my Comforter, I miss Dad
terribly now he has gone.

WHO ARE MY PARENTS?

My Saviour, I am full of sadness tonight
as I search through my situation.
Can I call her a mother
who held me in her womb and then gave me away?
Can I call him a father
who fathered me, then jilted my mother?
Can I call her a mother
who found another man, moved in with him,
leaving me behind?
Can I call him a father
who preferred another woman, set up home with her,
and promptly forgot me?
Can I call her a mother
who did not protect me from my father's anger
and aggression . . .
who stood and watched and whimpered
while I was beaten and threatened?
Can I call him a father
who misused his position of power and authority
to lash out at me, or to procure me
for his own sexual satisfaction?
Can I call her a mother
who did not call the police or alert a neighbour?
Can I call him a father
who drank and gambled and spent all our money
and never sought help?
Are they my parents
who signed me into care,
or who dumped me with a relative,
or who handed me over to foster-parents,
or who filled in adoption papers?
They chose a stranger to complete
the job that they had begun.

When I was terrified,
they left me to cry all alone.
I ask You, my Saviour,
is there anyone who cares enough about me?
If these are not my parents . . .
Who *are* my parents?

I ENVY MY BROTHER

Envy might not be the best feeling to have –
but I'm full of envy towards my brother.
Where there is a favourite, I'm looked down upon;
Where there is a layabout, I do all the hard work;
Where there is a superior, I'm the underdog;
Where there is a traitor, I can be relied upon;
Where there is a liar, I tell the truth.
In this house, I'm the person taken for granted;
I'm the person blamed for everything that goes wrong;
I'm the person always told to calm down;
I'm the person expected to try harder at school.
That makes me always 'on trial',
always here on sufferance,
always having to prove myself.
Although I am housed here, I am homeless.
Although I was born into a family,
I am basically unloved.
I see someone, perhaps younger,
getting all the treats;
I see someone, perhaps less brainy,
getting top marks;
I see someone who's far less adaptable
being praised for coming to terms
with my stubbornness!
O, my Comforter,
this all makes me confused.
I sense injustice;
I sense neglect;
I sense that my special needs
are being overlooked.
My little star has been eclipsed
so that a brighter star can shine;
I have been passed over

so that this rocket can be launched;
I am unheard
so that this other voice can speak.
Yet I know that envy is sinful,
and self-defeating;
I know envy will eat me up
before it conquers my rival.
Is this what I really want?

I CAN'T GET ON WITH MY STEPSISTER

I'm here, my Friend,
because I can't get on with my stepsister
even though we have known each other
for months.
I am beginning to wonder
whether the situation ever will get better . . .
whether I shall become more generous,
more understanding, more thoughtful,
more sympathetic, more talkative.
Perhaps my stepsister will become more reasonable,
more polite, more unselfish,
more discreet, more outgoing.
If new relationships need working on,
then we have the time – if not the will –
to grow closer.
Until now, I always thought of relatives
as people who lived *outside* our home.
Now I realise that some relatives
can decide to move *into* our home,
responding to their father's invitation.
Suddenly I have a sister figure
who was not born to my father and my mother.
Suddenly I have here another person –
who wants a bedroom, who wants attention,
who wants protection, who wants *affection* . . .
who also – though she may not realise it – wants the
    best deal.
All could have been ours – and ours alone –
as a natural family, if only we had not a mother
who decided to form a composite family . . .
with all that shallow talk about extra children to
'cement' the new relationship.
Children moving out . . .

children moving in . . .
fresh children conceived.
It's all getting like a nursery
in the first week of a new year.
It is almost too late for me to protest . . .
except to You.

WHY DO SO MANY CHILDREN LIVE HERE?

O God,
why do so many children live here?
They are all around me.
Other people's houses are fairly empty;
ours is crammed full.
Other people get their homework
and revision done in peace . . .
That is impossible here.
Other people get showered
with gifts and treats and gadgets.
There would not be enough money
for things like that here.
I can't even invite a close friend round,
or to stay the night.
Children and adolescents
crowd into our bathroom
as if waiting for a pantomime to begin.
Perhaps we *are* all like the cast of a pantomime:
jostling and apeing,
screaming and playing about.
It is enough to frighten most other teenagers away!
I hate having bunk-beds piled on top of one another
as if I was serving in the Navy;
I hate having feeble rations dished out
as if I'd been conscripted into the Army;
I hate having a rigid pecking-order
just like the command of the Air Force.
I cannot understand what possessed my parents
to bring so many children into the world
and to gather us into one bickering brood.
I cannot see the point of making
ordinary homes like ours into
Butlins by the sea.

Somehow, Saviour, rescue me . . .
or at least give me more tolerance . . .
the ability to distance myself
from all that's happening around me.
Some days, help me to *enjoy*
all these extra bodies
which provide variety,
and take a lot of pressure off *my* back.

I NEED TIME AWAY FROM MY BROTHERS AND SISTERS

I have approached You before, my Friend,
about the trouble with my brothers and sisters.
It has led to the whole family acting differently.
I have told You about their personalities
and their peculiarities.
Sometimes I condemn them.
At other times I simply ignore them.
I now need a spell away from them,
(particularly from one of them).
Even if it is only for a few days or weeks,
I need time away from them
so that I can build up my reserves
and work out what is making me disturbed –
why I distrust them; why they distrust me.
There will have to be an end to our quarrelling . . .
so that none of us says we're right
and the others are wrong.
We must stop enjoying seeing each other punished.

I approached my parents some time ago
and asked for a separate bedroom.
I could do with a whole separate granny-flat
to sort myself out!
I pleaded for different meal-times,
for a portable TV,
and for a rota to cover our showers
and the tidying up.
I'd like a clear zone
so that I can spend a while on my own.
Or else I will keep on my headphones
most of the time – which my parents say is antisocial.
Cutting myself off must be in my mind

as well as with my body.
I know I need to keep a low profile
more days than I do already.
I know I should make more allowances,
stay cool, and not rise to the bait.
I know how I *should* behave towards them,
but I forget in the heat of the moment.

Perhaps, my Friend, I was never meant to be a hermit.
If I could get away from them more,
they might appreciate me more
when I am with them.

PART FIVE

BEYOND THESE WALLS

WHAT CAN I TELL MY FRIEND?

O Saviour,
I want to tell You what's on my mind.
I come to You
because I am hiding from a friend
what I really think,
where I really stand.
I see a friend putting on weight.
Should I tell her?
I see a friend going wrong.
Should I tell her?
I see a friend growing scruffy.
Should I tell her?
I have a friend who drinks too much.
Should I tell her?
I have a friend who smokes too much.
Should I tell her?
I have a friend who talks too much.
Should I tell her?
When my friend is lazy . . .
should I tell her?
When my friend tells lies . . .
should I tell her?

When my friend is spiteful . . .
should I tell her?
Should I tell a friend
who keeps borrowing money,
and frittering away money,
that she needs to be more careful?
Should I tell a friend
who is getting very depressed
and bottling up a lot of worries
and rushing round like a maniac
that she needs to confide in somebody?
Is it up to me to tell a friend what not to do?
Am I my friend's keeper?
Other friends keep asking me how much I know.
Is it my duty to tell them – or to keep quiet?
I try to be a good friend –
but sometimes I'm determined
to add my piece.
I try not to judge,
but I'm not very good at defending my friend.
I certainly know
how to live other people's lives.

O God, is there a right way . . . a right time?
How much can I tell my friend about me?
How much can I tell my friend about *her*?

MY FRIEND IS GOING THROUGH A DIFFICULT PATCH

I bring to Your notice today, my Saviour,
a friend who's going through a difficult patch.
He used to be fairly problem free . . .
but no longer.
He used to sail along in the breeze . . .
but no longer.
He used to belong to a lovely family . . .
but no longer.
Dark clouds now surround my friend.

These are some of the difficulties he now faces:

These are some of the ways he might need helping:

These are the ways *I* had thought of helping him:

O God, let Your love and tenderness be known to him.
Strengthen his resolve.
Lift his spirits.
Give him wisdom sorting out so many problems.
Guard him.
Guide him.
Keep him.
Feed him.
And – in the fullness of time –
according to Your purposes –
bring him from darkness into light.

I AM WORRIED ABOUT MY CIRCLE OF FRIENDS

O God, I have a circle of friends
who keep me thinking and praying.
There must be a reason
why friends come in circles:
circles of encouragement,
protection, endearment.
And when a circle is broken,
the whole draws closer – to leave no gap.
I want to be loyal to my circle of friends,
and not break out of the circle. . . .
Because I need them to be my friends.
We go out hunting in a pack.
People say: 'Why choose friends like that?'
'Why be troubled by friends like that?'
People expect you to become immersed
with friends who've got no spirit.
Adults even pretend
they are experts on friendship . . .
although their own friends
let them down often enough.
Parents *especially* pretend
they are experts on friendship –
although the strength of *their* partnership
is often in doubt.

I know about my circle of friends
because I am one of them.
I understand their tears and their laughter.
I hear their secrets and learn about their motives.
I join in their celebrations.
My circle of friends make allowances for me –
and I for them.
They forgive me when I do something stupid.

Even so, some of my friends, O God,
are worrying me.
They are drawing me a bit too far away
from my family . . .
a bit too far away from my ideals . . .
a bit too far
into places where I do not want to go.

Will I now find myself in another circle,
a circle which would run rings round me
without helping me at all?

I AM GROWING APART FROM MY BOYFRIEND

My Guardian, I come to you tonight
because I'll soon be finishing with my boyfriend.
I am always irritated
when a boy makes advances
without thinking of my mood or my willingness.
I am always exasperated when a boy
is possessive about me
as if I can't chat up other boys
or go out with *my* girlfriends . . .
or have an evening at home on my own.
I'm not an object –
something belonging to someone else.
I'm not a tart –
someone ready to go to bed with *any*one.
I don't want to rush into
an unsatisfactory relationship
or listen to the first person
who says he can't live without me.
Help me in this instance to say NO –
and then to say GOODBYE.
I did like him, but not now.

I AM GROWING APART FROM MY GIRLFRIEND

I'm growing apart from my girlfriend.
Our relationship is on the rocks.
I've had girlfriends before . . .
and the same thing happened.
Some days I really want to stick with this girl.
On other days, I am fed up with her.
It's very difficult to know *which* girl I like . . .
and which girl *really* likes me, my Saviour.
Meanwhile, I already have this girlfriend,
but we seem to be growing apart, like strangers.
We do share a few interests –
but *my* interests always come first.
When we go for a night out,
she enjoys herself more than me.
I'm not very committed –
because of what I could be doing without her.
So I paddle on the edge of fondness
without diving in.
I hear rumours
that my girlfriend has found someone else.
I hear suggestions
that we never look like 'a couple'.
This makes me want to confront her . . .
but what's the point
when she smiles and says: 'Everything's all right'?
Everything is *not* all right –
or I wouldn't be thinking so hard.
Perhaps we both wanted to get too serious too early.
Perhaps we had closeness without warmth,
looks without love.
If we split, we'd be
glad of all we have shared . . .
knowing so much more for next time.

WHERE DID MY LOVE LIFE GO WRONG?

They told me: 'Unlucky in cards, lucky in love!'
Where did my love life go wrong?
They told me: 'Faint heart never won fair lady.'
Is that where my love life went wrong?
They told me: 'Everyone loves a lover.'
Where did my love go wrong?
They told me: 'Love bears all things,
hopes all things, endures all things.'
Is that where my love life went wrong?
They told me: "Tis better to have loved and lost
than never to have loved at all.'
Where did my love life go wrong?
They told me: 'Man dreams of fame
while woman wakes to love.'
Is that where my love life went wrong?
They told me: 'Love does not dominate;
it cultivates.'
Where did my love life go wrong?
They told me: 'When we are in love,
we often doubt what we most believe.'
Is that where my love life went wrong?
They told me: 'The magic of first love
is our ignorance that it can ever end.'
Where did my love life go wrong?
They told me: 'Perfect love never settles
in a light head.'
Is that where my love life went wrong?
They told me: 'Love comes in at the window
but goes out at the door.'
Where did my love life go wrong?
They told me: 'Love is blind.'
Is that where my love life went wrong?

O Comforter, love *brings* love while separation
leads only to alienation.
I have tried to translate
the love in my heart into reality –
but reality has proved too harsh
to sustain the love in my heart.
Faced with comparison, my love life
is barren, confused, farcical.
At least Scripture tells me: 'God is love;
whoever dwells in love, dwells in God.'

I BROKE WITH MY BEST FRIEND TODAY

I did not go to bed last night intending
to break with my best friend.
I did not wake up this morning
thinking about a split . . .
but I've now broken off from my best friend.
In a torrent of harsh words,
with a mixture of tears and self-righteousness,
with feelings of pain tinged with anger,
I have told her I will see her no more.
I was brave.
I said it outright.
I made sure she got the message.
I pretended I would have no regrets . . .
but it is because I have all those regrets *now*
that I come back to You, my Comforter.
I have had an hour or two to think it over.
I have gone over our parting words many times.
I have rehearsed what each said to each –
and I have remembered all I *meant* to say,
but failed to say.
Isn't it strange how very important words
stay clear in my mind,
so that my last memory of this friend
will be a very unhappy split,
not the hundreds of happy days
we enjoyed together up until today . . .
when we came to know each other,
when we were bonded together like glue,
when we promised we would be friends
for ever.
I have broken with friends before –
but not with a friend so near . . .
and *when* I have broken with friends before,

there has always been
a way of repairing the damage,
and healing the split.

Tonight I do not know whether pride
or principle stops me making it up.
I fear this split might be permanent.
For all I know, she might already
have looked for an alternative friend . . .
whilst I can't see a time
when I'd ever begin that search.
Perhaps I'll put the whole sorry story
on one side till another day.

I AM BORED AT SCHOOL

When I look at a text book,
I flick through its pages;
When I look at an exercise book,
I doodle in it;
When I look at the blackboard,
I study the teacher's clothing.
I look beyond the OHP screen
to the corner of the playing-field.
I can't get started on the lists or graphs
or charts or dates or maps I'm set –
nor can I even find a title for my essay.
I am bored at school: thoroughly bored –
bored when we have our regular teacher . . .
bored when we have a Supply;
bored during assembly;
bored during registration;
bored queueing for dinner;
bored hanging round after dinner;
bored reading; bored writing;
bored in maths . . .
bored learning languages;
bored singing songs.

My Guide, I don't think that they planned schools
to take account of me;
I don't think they planned lessons
to take account of *my* interests.
I don't think school is teaching me
what I'll need in later life.
But I'm sure it would teach me what my teachers
were taught in their early lives . . .
if only I listened . . .
if only I stopped being bored.

Boredom has its advantages, of course.
Boredom saves me from having to commit myself.
Boredom keeps me from cramming up my mind
with facts I won't need.
I can be physically in the classroom –
but mentally out of it.
I can pretend to be following instructions
when really I am following my instincts –
my instinct to be anywhere else
but sitting in a little cell
leading off from a long corridor –
just like a prison!

I AM BEHIND WITH MY SCHOOLWORK

I'm worried about my schoolwork.
I'm falling behind.
I used to try harder.
Yet they always said: 'Could try harder'!
Now I'm behind with my project.
I'll have to do a rushed job on that;
by copying chunks out of a book
and adding magazine photos.
But You know it will be a rotten project.
And I've got mountains of homework to finish.
I keep putting it off . . .
then I say it's gone missing.
One day I want to write a very unusual essay,
a memorable poem.
One day I want my work read out to the whole class . . .
but for the time being, I'm simply getting by . . .
trying to get through each tedious school day.
I know my teachers are disappointed.
I know my parents are disappointed.
But You will always understand –
understand that my mind is on other things just now.
Before all these exams, I *should* be revising.
I should be learning everything I am supposed to know.
But I can't concentrate.
I daydream at home, and I daydream at school.
I can manage a few uncertainties, my Friend . . .
but not so many uncertainties all at once.
On my way to school, my thoughts are somewhere else.
At school, my thoughts are somewhere else.
On my way home from school,
my thoughts are somewhere else.

One day – my Friend – it will all catch up with me . . . .

I'll tear up all my exercise books
and fail all my exams.
That'll be the end of it . . .
when everyone will know.
Yes: I'm worried about my schoolwork.

WE ALL MESS ABOUT IN CLASS

O God, I have a class to learn with:
a class to learn *within*.
I have a class which is supposed
to be learning something –
but it *doesn't* and I don't either.
My class doesn't want teaching –
or learning.
My class doesn't want writing to do –
or anything to do.
My class doesn't want topics to discuss –
or anything to discuss . . .
except subjects of *its own* choosing
when all heads should be bowed.
My class doesn't want to concentrate –
so it goes on strike: not militantly,
with banners and pickets.
My class goes on strike
by simply never beginning the work.
It is so easy to lay down tools
if you've never taken them up.
My class makes a lot of noise
for such a small number of people.
That noise is loud enough
to drown any outside voices –
like the teacher's voice
or the principal's voice.
My class makes up a lot of jokes
for such a small number of comedians.
Then, there is all the movement.
Everybody moves to and fro,
shuffling and crawling.
Our movement has nothing to do with learning
because our class has nothing to do with learning.

Sometimes objects are thrown
across the room and out of the windows.
We are lucky to have a class clown,
with trifle all over his face.
We are lucky to have a class cheerleader;
she helps us all to jeer.
I'm part of that class, my Friend,
but I'm not always at ease in that class.
I would cut myself off from that class,
but I haven't got the courage to . . .
because this class still recognizes me
as one of themselves.
I need to be part of my class
because I've not been told
to be part of any other class.
Please can I be part of *Your* class
even when I am in the midst of all the action
– or inaction – in my own class.

I AM BEING BULLIED AT SCHOOL

They told me
there were no bullies at our school . . .
that bullying had been wiped out.
They told me that our school
had an excellent reputation . . .
a proud record of good staff/student
and student/student relations.
They told me students worked
happily together
in drama, human movement,
class-work and computer graphics.
And I believed that I would be safe . . .
to enjoy some of the happiest days of my life.
Instead,
these past few months have been among
the most miserable of my life.
I have been teased in ways
I do not think are funny.
I have been taunted in ways
I do not think are fair.
I have been tormented in ways
I do not think are forgivable.
I have lost my kit, my bag and baggage . . .
and my self-confidence.

I am clever enough.
Perhaps that is a threat
to less academic students.
I am sporting enough to have a go
at most games . . .
Perhaps that is a challenge
to students determined to win.
I am tall enough . . .

so bullying does not only happen to weak people.
I am fashionable enough.
So bullying does not pounce only on the rag-bag . . .
only on the odd-ball.

Perhaps there is something
in my attitude or my beliefs,
my voice, or my self-presentation
that does not conform
to other people's expectations.
Perhaps I have broken group rules and
(so far) resisted group pressures.

I do not want to stay away from school
because of the bullies.
I do not want to answer back,
or to run away from the bullies.
Maybe I should stand still
until the storm passes over.
I have a Protector in You.

I AM ADDICTED TO GAMING MACHINES

They told me there'd be flashing lights,
music, warmth, bleeps, zaps, cascades . . . fun.
They told me there'd be no admission fee.
'Just bring some two p. pieces', they said.
'Bring ten p., the odd one-pound coin.'
So I brought my pocket money along
and gave it all away.
They said I couldn't lose, only win . . .
win far more coins than I could ever lose –
win dozens of coins, all at once.
It was then I knew I was a sure winner
because I won ten ten p. pieces straightaway.
It was almost my first go . . .
and I beat the machine.
That gave me a thrill . . .
beating the machine.
I could even switch arcade
and beat a different machine.
Now I am thrilled every day.
I can't wait for lunch-time or after tea.
The arcade is still there when I am not there.
Other people are winning when I am not there – but
not winning as much as when I *am* there –
because I can win more . . . I'm *sure* I can win.

I *know* these machines. I know their moods.
I know when to play and when to quit . . .
when there's a jackpot and when there's a void.
You see, my Friend, I've met other punters.
They win sometimes when I have not won . . .
That makes me more determined to win next time –
because I always make an excuse to go back . . .
even when we're all on holiday together . . .

People ask me how I do it.
They are knocked back by the risks I take.
But I never say how much I *lose*,
because I have lost everything, and still I lose.

Because I've lost all sense,
Arcadia is now my Hell.

SHOULD I GO TO THIS PARTY?

O God, should I go to this party?
The last party I went to made me very miserable.
I drank too much,
then at midnight I left for the chippie.
Then I was sick all over the pavement.
The party before that, I stayed till dawn broke.
My parents were away.
That was fun.
I want to say NO to this invitation:
   NO to the loud music;
   NO to the gate-crashers;
   NO to the billowing smoke of cigarettes;
   NO to the screaming and the calling;
   NO to the kissing and fumbling.
I want this time to stay sober . . .
but I do not know how to stay that way
without saying NO.
I'm bound to offend the person who's invited me.
It was supposed to be a great celebration:
somebody's birthday.
It was to be a house-warming, the heart-warming chance
to let our hair down, to put on silly dress . . .
a chance to forget the dullness of a world
that goes round far too slowly . . .
beneath coloured lights that go round so fast.
Perhaps I should go along after all —
to show that excitement is different from excess.
And to look for You through every door.

PART SIX

TOUGH QUESTIONS

POLLUTION IS GETTING WORSE

O God, I want to understand how serious pollution is . . .
and it is getting worse.
Pollution is like one huge avalanche –
an avalanche of poisonous chemicals
and indestructible plastics;
an avalanche of nuclear fall-out
and noxious fertilizers;
an avalanche of sewage and slurry.
This avalanche rushes towards me
guided in its path
by thousands of used rubber tyres.
This avalanche threatens to destroy
everything of beauty
on land and in the sea.
This avalanche cannot be stopped by me alone,
by the local council,
or by *one* industry setting a good example.
O, Thou Friend of the Earth,
sit down with us,
and direct all our deliberations.

NOBODY SEEMS TO CARE ABOUT THIS NEIGHBOURHOOD

O God, I come to You today
asking You to visit this neighbourhood . . .
transforming those parts which are ugly,
preserving the character and buildings
of the good parts.
My immediate neighbourhood is quite small.
There's our house, next door's,
this road and a few surrounding streets.
You could walk every inch of this neighbourhood
in half a day,
with time in hand to retrace your steps.
Why, if it's so small, does nobody care about it?
Why does no councillor do something about the mess?
Where is the tenants' association?
Doesn't the town hall have an inspector?
I could take You to a different neighbourhood
a mile or two further on —
where everybody is proud to live . . .
where councillors *did* do something about the mess,
where there *was* an active tenants' association,
and where officials from the town hall
did use their powers.

Why not here?
Who will ever care for *this* neighbourhood?
Will the interest have to spring from within *me*?

THE CHALLENGE OF FUND-RAISING

Outside Charity's door we leave our boxes . . .
glad to have collected these coins on her behalf.
Gathering all this money in has been hard work
made easier by the way we have worked
so closely together
promoting every good cause.
In our walking, climbing, and bed-pushing,
we have been sponsored.
We have counted peas in a jar
and marbles in a saucepan.
We have sold our parents' white elephants
and got our parents to dip their hands in a bran-tub.
In Charity's honour we have baked our cakes . . .
for her we have torn off raffle-tickets
and bought lottery-tickets.
At some houses we have left little envelopes;
in other houses we have done little jobs.
We have sung; we have danced for Charity.
And after we have guessed the weight of a sheep,
in Charity's name we have roasted it on a spit.
The blind now see; the lame now walk.
The lifeboat is launched; penguins are preserved.
New hospices open their doors
as old orphanages shut theirs.
Our money does good wherever it lands.
Charity is happy and we are happy.
She asked for our time; we gave it.
She asked for our compassion.
And we did what we could.
When Charity emerges, so do we.

MEN AND WOMEN

O God, women still fall so far behind men.
And girls fall so far behind boys.
Mothers suffer at the hands of fathers.
Schoolgirls stand around in corridors outside
watching schoolboys hogging computers inside.
Priests lead great religious processions
hardly noticing the women bringing up the rear.
Men deliver their speeches
refreshed by women laying on tea and cakes.
Managers still belittle manageresses.
Actors still upstage actresses.
Male sport fills every available television slot.
Whilst all the time
male moods attract fear and admiration;
female moods only attract pity and ridicule.
And when we address You, Our God,
we still talk in masculine terms –
Father, Almighty, King, Master of Mankind.
We said we'd aim for sexual equality . . .
so that women can do all the housework
and ask men to assist;
so that women can care for elderly folk
and ask men to stand by;
so that women can bring up the nation's children
and ask men to read them bedtime stories.

O God, help us to study our opposites
and to mean what we say about equal
treatment and equal treats.

THE FORGOTTEN PEOPLE

They found the body of a traveller today
in the boiler-house of a school;
they found the body of a tramp today
huddled beneath a railway arch;
they found the body of an alcoholic today
lying flat out on a park bench;
they found the body of a missing teenager today
still wrapped in its cardboard box;
they found the body of an old woman today
in the corner of a multi-storey car-park;
they found the body of a young prostitute today
behind the screens of the cricket pitch;
they found the body of a drug addict today
surrounded by needles and sugar-lumps
and polythene bags;
they found the body of Christ today
hanging on a Cross.

And some of these bodies they carried away
and some they left undisturbed.
A few of these bodies showed signs of life . . .
They had not died yet; they meant to arise . . .
And to haunt those who worried
only when they moved . . .
and those who passed by
when they didn't move.

O God, when *You* found our bodies
were our hearts already frozen?

NO PLACE LIKE HOME

O God, some subjects are so huge . . .
we would rather not think about them at all.
Take homelessness.
We want the Government to think about it,
or the town hall;
or social workers;
or Probation;
or the Salvation Army;
or the Police.
Not us. Not yet.
Because we *have* homes to go out from
and homes to come back to.
We were promised shelter
from when we were born.
Or were we?
We could be homeless any day now . . .
If the mortgage falls into arrears;
If our parents divorce;
If our homes are burnt down or bombed;
If those who keep our homes lose their jobs –
Or if other debts pile up.
We should then be homeless
crowded in one dingy Bed and Breakfast room,
or one caravan . . .
with no privacy, no belongings,
no kitchen of our own –
cast aside and bundled about
by the society that claimed to care about its young.
O God, Protector, protect now
those families cruelly thrown out of their homes –
told to leave the security of their boarded-up houses
to face the insecurity of boarding houses . . .
And let us never rest till they too can rest assured.

FED UP WITH HUNGER

I am worn out with caring.
I have seen the starving millions:
ribs poking out of their chests,
legs bowed, hands outstretched.
They too are worn out with caring.
They have seen our bloated executives:
bulging wallets poking out of their chests,
diet-sheets in hand,
heads turned the other way.
Our caring troubles them
because it runs out too soon.
We send a few sacks of grain
which run out too soon.
We send a few boxes of pills
which run out too soon.
But our caring also prompts us
to build modern chemical works.
We send all makes of weapon –
which widen tribal differences.
We send cigarettes which will feed nobody.
We send powdered milk which will nourish no baby.
Then we send motor cars,
to keep our motor industry at full capacity.
Even when we send cash,
it is in the form of tied loans,
each carrying high rates of interest,
to deepen Third World debt.
We feed few bodies; we feed few minds . . .
O God, how shallow is our caring.

EARTHQUAKE ZONE

There's been an earthquake.
After all, it was an Earthquake Zone.
Thousands are reported dead . . .
their country an Earthquake Zone.
Hundreds of thousands are homeless . . .
their homes in an Earthquake Zone.
Medicines have been flown out . . .
scarce in an Earthquake Zone.
Startling images are captured on film . . .
straight from an Earthquake Zone.
Survivors sleep uneasily in their tents . . .
camped out in that Earthquake Zone.
Soldiers dig deep in the rubble . . .
piled high on that Earthquake Zone.
Little children are wandering about . . .
unschooled in an Earthquake Zone.
Distraught mothers cry for their babies . . .
born to die in an Earthquake Zone.
Nightmares haunt those who are left . . .
to survey the Earthquake Zone.
The shops which remain are looted.
Who buys, in an Earthquake Zone?
No new crops will be planted . . .
for harvesting an Earthquake Zone.
Millions of pounds have been raised . . .
in aid of that Earthquake Zone.
Billions of pounds will be needed . . .
to rebuild the Earthquake Zone.
O God what forces were active . . .
beneath this Earthquake Zone?
Creator of all creation
hear our prayers for each Earthquake Zone.

PART SEVEN

EACH DAY OF THE WEEK

MONDAY

As I come to You today,
I reflect on how a dentist's surgery might be.
I see a cluster of men and women and children
sitting round in a circle . . . waiting to go in –
not wanting to go in . . .
not even wanting to be there . . .
but there for a purpose,
there for a short spell of unpleasantness
to avoid many more days of pain and misery.
Each customer nervously eyes the others.
Few are concentrating on the array of magazines!
Along the passageway the dentist is at work:
arc lights are glaring;
and scrapers are scraping.
Eyes are screwed up in agony –
everyone pledges never to come back.

So I stood as I approached another Monday.
I did not want the ordeal . . .
and I tried to escape it.
I looked round nervously

and discovered that my friends felt the same as I did.
I did not want the drill that drilled deep . . .
nor the scraper that scraped at my inadequacy . . .
nor pliers that plucked out my most persistent
    obsessions.
I did not want any moments of unpleasantness
even if there were happier days ahead.
Nor did I want Your arc light
lighting up my unkindest instincts,
my unhealthiest appetites.
Sometimes it is I who rejoice
at the hardships that others face . . .
whilst I postpone my appointment before You.

TUESDAY

This morning, as I prepare for another day,
I reflect on how a factory might be.
Overnight its store-rooms have been replenished;
its aisles and walkways have been swept clean.
Great machines stand motionless,
Long conveyor-belts rest on their rollers,
Heavy lifting-gear hangs from the gantries overhead,
Trolleys hover beside well-worn work benches.
The order-book is full but the cloakroom is empty.
Soon all that will change: men and women
will climb out of trains and buses.
Some will walk whilst others will run,
afraid of the penalty of failing to clock in on time.
Then each one will stand in the appointed place,
to feed the machines; to operate them;
to mend the machines; to check the product.

So shall I stand in the factory of life today . . .
completing work schedules, producing ideas.
I am idle now . . . but not for long.
The clock will strike soon, and my shift will begin.
Your energy will start up my machinery.
Your protective shield will guard my efforts.
Doubtless at times I shall grind to a halt,
and need You to reset me.
Then shall I be happy to take
all that comes from my hand or brain
and show it to You . . . faultless, untarnished.
My life might look like a plain shed from outside . . .
But You know my inner workings,
and they are special.

WEDNESDAY

I come to You today, Saviour,
as I might in my imagination approach
a big railway station:
some trains are hauled by big locomotives,
others by smaller engines.
Some trains are about to begin long journeys –
passing through complex junctions and great cities;
other trains will take people on shorter journeys –
to quiet country villages and market towns.
There are announcers and announcements
as departure boards rattle and rotate
according to some master-plan,
some detailed timetable.
Little kiosks sell tea and sandwiches;
others sell tickets, tapes and ties.
Homeless people rise wearily from fixed benches.
All around is hustle and bustle.
So I stand where important decisions are made
and previous plans are altered, and
I get up to be noticed by my fellow-travellers.
So begins my journey through the day.
I hear announcements loud and clear:
some significant, others quite meaningless . . .
and I must decide which are which before I start out.
Sometimes I shall be pulled from up front;
sometimes I shall be pushed from behind –
yet all through today
I shall be safely guided along life's way
towards the destination which is this evening –
according to Your great purposes,
Your timing, Your provision. Thank You.

THURSDAY

Today as I come to You, O God,
it is as if I am surrounded by books
in a second-hand bookshop.
Little stairways lead off into alcoves and anterooms.
Floor-to-ceiling shelves are crammed with books:
heavy books and light books,
heavy reading and light reading.
Some books I see have been thrown away
by their owners as useless –
their libraries broken up;
other books are much sought after by collectors.
Here and there are cardboard boxes
overflowing with books not yet sorted.
Every book tells its own tale: the tale
of a child who learnt to read,
of a mother who rested from her chores . . .
of an author who wrestled for years to set out
ideas, research findings, propositions, for future ages.
So I stand – surrounded by the nooks
and crannies of my life.
My mind overflows with discarded knowledge –
and with ideas and dreams yet to be sorted.
When I was young I spoke simply;
When I began to study, I learnt to speak wittily;
One day I shall speak with authority –
but every day I shall need to rest my mind.
That way I shall not gather dust – or fall apart –
like so many ancient volumes.
Grant that my beliefs, my personality,
my occupations, are forever gathered in One Place,
that they be not broken up.

FRIDAY

O God, my thoughts tonight take me to a cinema.
There is a major film, and clever adverts.
There are noisy latecomers, shown in
by an usherette with wavering torch.
Some people unwrap sticky sweets
while others poke at ice cream.
I wonder at why people go to the cinema
when they could watch all their films at home . . .
Perhaps they go for the sense of occasion;
perhaps for the breadth of vision;
perhaps for concentration uninterrupted;
or for the sharpness of the action,
and the underlying emotions.
So I stand in a celluloid world that is
both totally artificial and amazingly real –
as films are projected so many frames each minute.
Each frame is lifeless, pointless,
until it is powerfully lit from behind.
My life has its main action outdoors
whilst the supporting action is indoors.
My days allow for totally artificial experiences
and those which are real.
My days – like a film –
are not over till I have advertised myself . . .
People come into my life,
and leave it, sometimes at the wrong moments.
They are extras in my film, and late-comers.
If today lacked a sense of occasion
and a depth of vision,
perhaps I did not let Your light shine
strongly behind me.

SATURDAY

It is strange, my Friend, to have a day
which is not already planned for me.
I see myself in a huge department store
where thousands of customers will shop today.
Glass doors part for rushing footsteps.
Between five floors escalators
are in perpetual motion.
Cabinets display cutlery and crockery,
cameras and curtain-hooks.
An acre of floorspace is devoted to cosmetics:
perfumes and powders, lipsticks and lotions
– the beauticians serenely guard their wares.
Tidy plastic men wear made-to-measure suits.
Two floors higher, hundreds of rolls
of carpeting and cushionlay
wait to be rolled out.
This store no longer expects coinage,
just cheques and credit cards.
Help is there if you ask,
not always *when* you ask for it.
So I stand utterly bewildered by life's many choices:
choice of employment, choice of leisure . . .
choice of coat, choice of fragrance . . .
choice of habitat, choice of diet.
Sometimes the waiting is taken out of my wanting . . .
at other times, I am wanting more than I need.
But why do You leave me to *search*, to go
here and there for what I am looking for?
Shall I approach You first for assistance?

SUNDAY

This, O God, is the most solemn of days:
a chance to reflect on Your mercies and majesty.
In Church I enter by the porch
beyond the graves, the grass and the gravel,
the grievances, grudges and ingratitude
of every day.
I walk down the aisle
in a special act of witness.
I sit in a pew shaped differently
from other seats where I sit.
I sing hymns and psalms of praise
which do not sound the same as other songs.
I hear a sermon that does not sound
the same as other talks, other lectures.
A time soon comes for me to approach the altar –
'Do This In Remembrance of Me'.
Bright sunshine lights up the stained glass.
That *helps* my worship.
A gold cross glints above choirstalls.
That *helps* my worship.
Flowers decorate the ledges and the transept.
That *helps* my worship.
Candles flicker, first tentatively,
then glowingly, in a way that helps my worship.
Carved faces of the saints
surround the pulpit –
O God, I worship You with my whole heart.

NOW I CAN LIVE A HAPPIER LIFE

Now I can live a happier life.
All my thoughts I have brought before You;
All my hopes I have set in front of You;
All my anxieties I have left beside You;
All my doubts I have expressed to You;
All my achievements I have displayed to You;
All my questions I have asked You;
All my loving will be blessed by You;
All my gifts will be accepted by You;
All my mistakes will be forgotten by You;
All my trust will be placed in You;
All my joy will begin in You;
All my peace will be found in You.

>   Now I will
>   Be still . . .
>   Stay still . . .
>   Listen still . . .
>   Pray still
>   Until
>   I find it.

CONCLUSION

SEEK HELP WHERE YOU MAY FIND IT

If you have found these meditations helpful, you may wonder where to go from here.

Meditation can go a long way toward expressing the concerns on your mind, and some way toward solving problems. But apart from prayer and worship, you may need to seek additional support, and expert advice.

The telephone is useful. The Samaritans have a long and proud record befriending young people. You do not *have* to think of suicide before you contact them. More recently, CHILDLINE has come onto the scene. Its counsellors are far more in touch with teenage dilemmas than commercial chat-line operators.

Some branches of RELATE (formerly Marriage Guidance) are anxious to help teenagers with relationship difficulties, and many young people are fortunate in having very approachable family doctors. If you are unhappy with your family doctor, ask for a new doctor. Girls may feel easier talking to women doctors.

Other people are provided with form tutors, college course co-ordinators and lecturers ever ready to listen to problems arising both inside and outside the educational set-up.

Then, in the evenings and at weekends, youth and community leaders and youth club assistants are available for a chat. They have observed a lot, can share many insights and are often very approachable.

A common misunderstanding is that vicars, ministers, priests and deacons will only help churchgoers. We are seeing the rapid disappearance of church youth groups for 'church members or their families only'. Seek out your minister for both confession and guidance. S/he will not gobble you up – or criticise you. And if s/he is too busy, or not well up on your dilemma, s/he will show you whom to approach next.

Parents, for many teenagers, are definitely *not* a first point of call. But have you tried a part-time parent, or the parent of one of your friends? If you live with a step-parent, have you considered that s/he might be as anxious to talk as you are?

Never bottle problems up by stuffing them down inside you. Later they will surface much worse than how they were! There is always someone who will listen. Everyone has confidences and surprisingly few people betray each other's confidences.

Beware of one trap, however. Never commit someone like a social worker to 'tell no one else'. That person might be demoted or dismissed for 'telling no one else'. Whoever you approach, it is wise first of all to set down ground rules. How much further will this matter be taken? If it *is* taken further, or to someone else, will anonymity be given you until you say your real name can be released? Total anonymity is one of the chief reasons why many people write first to Agony Aunts care of a newspaper or magazine.

Seek help where you may find it . . . and you will sleep much more easily in your bed.

If, after writing off for advice, borrowing books from the library, approaching brothers and sisters, uncles, aunts and friends, you would *still* like to meditate and to pray: go along to your nearest Christian bookshop. There are SPCK bookshops, CLCs, Scripture Unions and many other local ones. In addition, most cathedrals and many churches and chapels have bookstalls.

These are a few of the books I have found helpful in my life, but you will discover many more:

Prayers of Life by Michel Quoist
Epilogues and Prayers by William Barclay
Prayers for Young People by William Barclay
A Private House of Prayer by Leslie Weatherhead

Many people have also enjoyed and found useful the books of David Adam: *The Edge of Glory, The Cry of the Deer, Tides and Seasons* and *The Eye of the Eagle*, with their use of Celtic themes; or Joyce Huggett's books about praying: *Listening to God* and *Open to God*; or Frank Colquhoun's collections of short prayers, *Prayers for Today, Family Prayers* and *Parish Prayers*.

Seek help where you may find it . . . and you will wake refreshed in the morning.

The PRAYING WITH series

A series of books making accessible the words of some of the great characters and traditions of faith for use by all Christians.